TYEASHIA ANSLEY–HUGHES-NEELEY

THE UN-NOTICED

Published by Chosen Vessels Publishing & Entertainment (USA) Inc.
Jacksonville, Florida 32210 U.S.A.
First Printing July 2018

Copyright © 2018 - **Tyeashia Ansley Neeley**
All rights reserved
Chosen Vessels Publishing & Entertainment, Inc.

REGSTERED TRADEMARK
ISBN – 978-0-692-08287-4

Printed in the United States of America
Book Cover by: Oliviaprodesign
Co-Writer Doreen "Dee" C. Whitfield

PUBLISHER'S NOTE

Unnoticed is a book of fiction. Names, characters, places, and incidents either are the product of the author's imagination or are used fictitiously, and any resemblance to actual persons, living, or dead, business establishments, events, or locales is entirely coincidental.

Without limiting the rights under copyright reserved above, no part of this publication may be reproduced, stored in or introduced into a retrieval system, or transmitted, in any form, or by any means (electronic, mechanical, photocopying, recording, or otherwise) without the prior written permission of both the copyright owner and the above publisher of this book.

The scanning, uploading, and distribution of this book via the Internet or via any other means without the permission of the publisher is illegal and punishable by law. Please purchase only authorized electronic editions, and do not participate in or encourage electronic piracy of copyrighted materials. Your support of the author's rights is appreciated.

Foreword

Tyeashia Ansley's memoir, **Unnoticed**, is an inspiring and triumphant coming-of-age story of tenacity, hope and the gift of prophecy from the age of nine.

Tyeashia Ansley is a woman of great faith and a Prophetess. Her painful early life, however, was quite different. Tyeashia and her two siblings survived an abusive and painful childhood only to find themselves faced with the challenges of the foster-care system, unreliable relatives and intermittent homelessness in the shadows of Baltimore Maryland and Jacksonville, Florida.

Based on a true-life abused-to-healed story, *The Unnoticed* chronicles Tyeashia's rising above her past, hearing the voice of God while fighting to keep her two sisters together through it all.

Sexual abuse of a child by a trusted adult puts tremendous strain on relationships within the family. Some family members may find it hard to believe the abuser could do such a thing and take sides (or feel pressured to take sides) over who is telling the truth. Family members may also struggle with how to manage their divided loyalties toward the abuser and the victim. Even in families that accept that the abuse occurred, reactions to the abuser may run the gamut from "lock him up and throw away the key" to "hate the sin but love the sinner." Tensions may arise when different family members have different opinions about loyalty, fairness, justice, forgiveness, and responsibility.

Beautifully written, with heartbreaking honesty, *Unnoticed* is an unforgettable reminder that regardless of the challenges and obstacles we face the God we serve will never leave us nor forsake us. And healing, forgiveness, and love are still within reach for those who have the faith, desire and the determination to trust and believe. ~

Dee C. Whitfield, Publisher

Acknowledgments

I would like to give thanks to God who is the head of my life for allowing this project to come to fruition. ***"His ways are not our ways."*** Therefore, this writing has been allowed to acknowledge the spiritual evidence of mine and my sibling's mother's death. We honor her life with this book of spiritual truths in love. I know her spirit smiles down upon us knowing we have not forgotten the love and care she had for us as her daughters on earth.

I thank my Aunt/Mother ~ Harriet for raising us to the best of her ability ***"For such a time as then."***

To my sisters Anterrinia and Latoyia, your motivation to finish the vision that had been given to me is very much appreciated.

When people count you out, God has the spiritual "Hook Up" to get you through the toughest of times.

To my earthly father, I am blessed to have been born through your seed. Though the relationship has not been what a daughter would envision with her father. You have and continue to push me to my destiny in more ways than one. This book is one of the ways.

I am forever grateful to God for revealing the spiritual events of my mother's life and death. An ending of a life gone too soon. Yet, a legacy left through three daughters who understand that only God has the last word. I love and miss you,

Debbie Darlene Ansley.

Authors Note

This book is an account of a true story. The quotes used to compile the narrative were taken from court documents and police reports. Conversations portrayed in this book have been reconstructed using research and interviews. All of the dates and locations mentioned throughout are factual. However, names have been changed.

Many authors of fiction-based books have written stories in which their characters are different in several ways. In this book, you will read about three little girls who faced unchangeable adversity in their childhood and the one who rose above the pain to make a change. Many may not understand the concept of the book and many will be able to relate. The reason

I chose to release my thoughts and insights for the book was for others to hear the story and hopefully encourage women and younger girls to speak up and not allow the advice of people to dictate what stories can or cannot be told. Many stories that are written can be painful and challenging. Nevertheless, I've chosen to relate and release this story that I pray will make a positive outcome not only in my life, but the hidden pain for those who are silenced by fear.

Chapter 1

Discerning spirits are one of the amazing gifts of the Holy Spirit. My name is Ta'tianna. I'm the middle child of three girls. I never asked for this gift, but I wanted to know why, how and who murdered my mom. No mother would deliberately, kill herself, leaving three beautiful daughters for someone else to take care of. I couldn't and wouldn't believe it! I wanted answers, I wanted truth more than anything I wanted my momma. The latter, I would never have, but answers and truth I could receive through the Holy Spirit.

At the young age of seven-years-old, I received this amazing gift. A person who has the gift of discerning spirits is able to either sense or see things in the spirit realm. That means that they can sense or see demons and angels. A person with discerning spirits can also get insight and information about spiritual things affecting other people, such as if they are oppressed or have a demonic influence in or around their person.

This gift has helped me discover how my mother was murdered. I'm able to tell this story through the guidance of the Holy Spirit. This gift flows out of a healthy relationship with the Holy Spirit and is not something done in one's own power.

God has given each one of us gifts to use so that we might exercise them faithfully for the Kingdom of God. Yet so many of us have lost belief that we are even capable of having these amazing gifts. The gifts of the Holy Spirit are so special – something from our amazing Father who wants to share a piece of heaven with us right here on earth. Not every person will have discerning spirits or healing, or something that seems "important" but you will have a gift, and believe me, it is very valuable in the eyes of God. Every gift is used to build up, encourage, and help other people and should be used in doing so. Please do not believe the lies that you are not worthy of receiving these gifts, or that these gifts are scary or don't even exist. You were made for such a time as this and if you are reading this right now, then please know God is calling you out at this very moment to use the gift he has given you.

I am certainly grateful for using my gift to share this amazing story of heartbreak and healing.

Each of you should use whatever gift you have received to serve others, as faithful stewards of God's grace in its various forms. 1 Peter 4:10

Chapter 2

It was a humid, hot afternoon in May of 1987. It was the introduction of summer, just after the trees had completely released all of the pollen that colored the roof, sidewalks, and car-hoods with green dust. The smell of fried eggs and bacon hung like a cloud over the kitchen at 7844 Gregory Drive apartment #334.

My daddy walked towards the stove like an E-flat melody was being played inside of his shoes. He offered an empty plate. His approach seemed forceful with an air of humility, kind of like the deacon at church when he passed that offering plate to you on Sunday. My mother filled his plate with scrambled eggs, topped with four pieces of bacon along with two slices of semi-warm toast topped with grape jelly.

My daddy could eat, and I mean he ate like the lining of his stomach had been removed. He cracked a half-smile after his plate was filled and took a slow stroll over to the kitchen table. He sat down, lowered his head and said a prayer, a quick one. "Thank you, Jesus," and that was it.

He sprayed a cotton rag with the hoppes solution, attached to the cleaning rod and forced it into the barrel of the shotgun.

My parent's master bedroom was the crime scene. The police would want to know if this was a suicide where the victim and suspect were one in the same. If it was, then gunshot residue could easily be found on my mother's hand and the trajectory of the shot could be reconstructed by forensics. Or was the suspect the person that my mother had assumed would protect her from scenes like this one.

It was ninety degrees outside, but it was cold in that bedroom. A crime of passion always starts with a cold deceitful heart and an unsound mind. But what's worse is when it looks like it was planned. There is nothing passionate about murder. Anger has no passion its codeword is rage.

One blast shook the bedroom. Twelve-gauge pellets littered the wall next to the eastside window of the room as they drove small chunks of my mother's face into the sheetrock. Blood covered the area around my mother's body like red syrup. My daddy glanced down at the human target that lay dead on the floor next to the queen-sized bed in front of him. He did a visual check of the room, making sure that it didn't show signs of a struggle. He had to think, and I mean in a hurry.

The human brain ain't wired on how to redirect evidence away from the real killer on a moment's notice. The mind needs a bit of time if you want it done right. But time was not one of the cards on the table. My daddy had three things working against him at the time of my mother's death: A dead body, a firearm in close proximity, and a black man were at the scene. Three cards that you never want to talk to the police about.

He shoved his hands down into his pants pockets and took a quick glance over his left shoulder making sure that one of his two daughters in the apartment wasn't standing in the doorway witnessing what had just happened. They were heavy sleepers, but he couldn't be sure that one of them hadn't got up to use the bathroom and inadvertently became a witness. His breathing thickened as he stared at the bedroom wall riddle with blood, brain matter and pellets from the gun blast. But one thing about every murder that is of great importance is the placement of the gun if there's one at the scene. Should you move it? Should you leave it where it is? The cops are going to know if that gun has been moved. They're going to know if that gun was against my mother's face when it was fired, or if there was clearance between her face and that barrel. That's what usually pokes a hole in your story. When the evidence doesn't line up with your statements is when everything starts to fall apart.

He had to move quickly. His children were in the house. He had to cook up a story and show some false sense of agony and despair when he walked into our bedroom so my sisters at one and three years old could tell the cops how distraught he looked. In toddler terms "Daddy's crying," if that.

He still hadn't called 911. He had to wake my little sisters before he called the police. Thank God they were still asleep!

There are three of us, but only two of us were home that night. I wasn't there. I am the middle child.

One at a time, he leaned over and shook my sisters firmly from their late evening slumber. Thirty-one years later my sisters remembered how his touch felt, like a bee sting when he shook them. My baby sister's neck retracted back into the pillow and her head lunged forward. She was in a deep sleep. But he needed them both to wake up in a hurry.

*You belong to your father, the devil, and you want to carry out your father's desires. He was a murderer from the beginning, not holding to the truth, for there is no truth in him. When he **lies**, he speaks his native language, for he is a liar and the father of **lies**. John 8:44*

Chapter 3

My mom loved decorating and our room was no exception. She purchased for us pretty, white, matching twin beds. The baby girl always ended up in one of the beds with my sister or me. For some reason, she never slept in her crib throughout the night.

A matching white dresser shared an uncovered pink and white polka dot, square, gift box of assorted ribbons and hair bows. We had an assortment of brown dolls sitting in my mom's favorite rocking chair. She would gather us onto her lap and read us stories. Rocking us back and forth. Sometimes we would fall asleep while she was reading.

The police report stated: two emptied 'Happy Meal' boxes sat in the center of the floor. One displayed a redheaded Ronald McDonald prize and a few French fries gone cold. We loved McDonald's and Happy Meals made us happy!

My dad, Andre' Anthony had spent his first four years in a common-law marriage with my mother, his then-girlfriend, Destiny, along with me and my two sisters his biological daughters, before giving up his single life to become a legal husband. He knew his side chicks were a force to be reckoned with.

Being married to your babies' momma wasn't a dream a street thug had. To give that up . . . to start the legal cohabitation life was something almost every thug avoided at all cost. A wifey on the surface was as legit as it was supposed to get. Not that he gave a flip about his side chicks. But he wasn't "Impulsive." The word my mother, Destiny had used. That was almost five years ago, and he had brushed her off at the time. Destiny didn't understand. He didn't expect her to. His thoughts were scattered, what had happened was surreal. He picked up the phone. He dialed 911 and told them his wife had killed herself. When he hung up he called his stepmom and told her he was on his way to her house. He would explain everything once he arrived. She was the only person he could talk to who would believe him and help him. He knew Destiny's family would try to get a death sentence for him once they found out she was dead.

He couldn't go back into the room where she lay. A sound from the refrigerator's icemaker dropping cubes clattered into the container holding them hostage until the release button freed them cube-by-cube.

1 Corinthians 7:9
*But if they cannot control themselves, they should **marry**, for it is **better to marry than to burn** with passion.*

Chapter 4

A stray drop of blood ran from her head and trickled across her cold caramel skin. Her body lay crumpled on the bedroom floor. A long sleeved blue scrub top clinging to her torso. She was titled on her side, her nude lower half, curled against the tiled floor.

The woman's drained of color face, beautiful - even in death. Blood from the brain wept into her dark brown hair. Jacksonville Police Officer P. L. Chauncey was midway through an uneventful Tuesday patrol shift when the call came in at 1:28 p.m. that a woman had been found unresponsive in her bedroom and had possibly committed suicide.

Tall and slender, with a shaven head and goatee, Officer Chauncey was dispatched to the scene. Flicking on his car's lights and sirens he sped toward the apartment complex. Turning down Wilson Boulevard, Chauncey pulled next to a curb outside apartment 7844 Gregory Drive #334 and parked behind another cruiser, its red and blue revolving lights still flashing. Chauncey's partner, Jay Newsom, had arrived just seconds of him in a separate car.

From the trunk of his cruiser Officer Chauncey grabbed a handheld mask ventilator---known as an Ambu bag he didn't know, he wouldn't need and followed Newsom up the natural rock steps and across the grassy front yard.

Knocking at the door delivered no response. Approximately 5 minutes later a car drove up and the victim's husband Andre Anthony got out. Mr. Anthony advised he lived in the apartment and that his wife had killed herself. At this point, Mr. Anthony unlocked the door, entry was made. Guiding the officers, Mr. Anthony said, "It's back there."

The victim was located in the northwest bedroom with what appeared to be a gunshot wound to the head.

As the two officers entered the bedroom, Chauncey's view was briefly obscured by his partner's broad build. Once Newsom stepped aside, Chauncey saw the woman lying on the blood-stained carpet. Chauncey's gaze fell to Andre Anthony, who had just rushed into the bedroom and kneeled next to his wife. Andre suddenly cried out in anguish. "All because of me coming home late?"

Why? Andre yelled. "Why did you have to do this? I told you to chill!"

Peering up, the two uniformed JSO officers exchanged a glance, Chauncey and Newsom walked over to the woman's side.

Mr. Anthony said, "I was trying to take the gun away from her when it discharged." Andre' blurted to the officers. "She was angry because I didn't come home last night. She became violent."

By this time rescue #8 personnel arrived and pronounced the victim dead.

"OK, Mr. Anthony," Officer Chauncey said, "I need to advise you of your constitutional rights." Andre sneered at the officer and said. "I already know them." Officer

Chauncey stated them clearly for the record. Andre loomed over his wife's body. "Why God? Why?" he cried.

Proverbs 29:10
Men of bloodshed hate the blameless, But the upright are concerned for his life.

Chapter 5

The bedroom was tidy and decorated with inexpensive African American art you purchased from Family Dollar, with large wooden dressers and an armoire holding a small television. A few decorated pillows were neatly arranged atop the queen size bed.

Stomping back in the bedroom, Andre looked up at the ceiling and cursed God. "After all we've been through. Why would you do this to me?"

Andre's increasingly aggressive outburst drew the attention of the officers. Struck by the man's animosity, Chauncey tensed, wondering if he would have to restrain Andre or defend himself. It was beyond the reaction of an anguished spouse and unlike anything, the officers had encountered.

Chauncey spoke first. "Mr. Anthony, we need to speak with you." Andre slowly moved away from his wife's body.

"He was very angry," Chauncey remembered years later. "It was uncomfortable, honestly, to have him come back and forth in the room yelling."

Officer Newsom pulled Andre aside. "Can you come with me, so we can gather more information?" The well-built veteran officer escorted Andre to the living room. As they spoke Andre offered various explanations for how and why his wife killed herself.

Andre took a deep breath and started sharing, "I stayed out all night and when I arrived home, she started in on me. Saying she was tired of being pushed around and she was depressed. I tried to ignore her and walked into the kitchen to fix me something to eat." He went on to say, "She flipped the script and said, "I'll fix breakfast. This is the only way you'll listen to me any way. I know you're probably hungry." "She's always been a good cook. She knew exactly how I liked my eggs. Over easy, not running. And the way she cooked grits ... Lord have mercy ... so creamy, never lumpy. She would use real butter, not margarine." He lowered his head and shook it. He seemed to be talking to no one in particular. Just reminiscing. "She cooked and talked. Saying she couldn't take being unappreciated and used. She set a plate on the placemat in front of me and slid the eggs onto the plate. I pretended to listen to her go on and on cause I wanted to eat. I was hungry as heck. When she reached for the pot of grits, I cringed wondering how to protect myself if she decided to throw them at me. She was just that angry." She said, "I'm not going to do this no more. My babies need us, but you ain't acting like you want to be with us! I'm not going to be the woman waiting for you to come home and everybody in the streets know I'm being cheated on. That won't work Andre!" He went on to say, "I ate in silence. I just wanted her to shut up and I hoped she would after eating some breakfast too. But she messed over the food and as you can see." He pointed to a plate that had barely been eaten from. Grits, eggs, and a half a slice of bacon sat mixed cold on a small plate.

He said, "She walked into the bedroom and started to pull clothes out of the dresser drawers saying she was leaving." I walked out of the room to check my beeper that kept beeping. I went back into the bedroom." He hesitated and continued. "When I walked in the room Destiny sat on the edge of the bed and held a shotgun in her hand. I tried to grab the shotgun. We struggled, and the gun discharged." He looked at Officer Newsom and said, "I panicked, and threw the shotgun over the balcony." He pointed to the balcony area. "Two of our daughters were home and asleep in their room. I went downstairs and retrieved the shotgun and placed it in the trunk of the car. I then called my stepmom to talk to her. When I hung up from her, I called 911. I woke my daughters up and carried them to the car." He began to talk in a whisper. "I took the shotgun to a wooded area to get rid of it."

Andre would not stop talking after being advised of his rights. He was extremely nervous. "Destiny's family don't like me. They gonna accuse me of killing her." He said. Officer Newsom asked, "Why is that?" We've had our share of ups and downs and she always ran to them when we had a fight." Officer Newsom continued to listen. "I went to my stepmoms after the shooting because she is the only person I felt I could go and get help."

Detective C.H. Parker ordered Officer Chauncey to transport Andre to the Homicide Division to be interviewed. Andre volunteered to take a polygraph examination that was scheduled for May 28th. Andre Anthony was booked in the Duval County jail for outstanding warrants and worthless checks.

Galatians 6:7
Do not be deceived: God cannot be mocked. A man reaps what he sows.

Chapter 6

As I am seeing my mother alive through the spirit realm I quietly watch her actions. My heart wanted to reach out and hug her. Tell her she's a *"great mommy"* and I would hold her until she takes her last breath. But, I'm only allowed to see what I have asked. I asked to witness how my mother died. How an outgoing, loving, twenty-four-year-old young woman suffering from low self-esteem and abuse supposedly kill herself. Both characteristics were delivered and received from my father's constant cheating and her inability to leave for the sake of her children.

Destiny's Thoughts

The air pulses as I am staring at the message on my husband's beeper, the beeper he carries around as if it were an instrument to keep him alive and holding our three-year-old screaming daughter Tina is on my lap, it's hard to breathe. He obviously forgot his beeper after taking a shower last night. He had recently purchased the latest version beeper or pager that allowed for a short 80-character text message. I read the first line of the message and bile begins to rise in my throat. I try to take a breath, but I can't get any air in. I have to breathe. And I have to make this baby stop crying before she wakes my other baby. This has to be a misunderstanding. As soon as I can talk to Andre, he will explain because I'm pissed, and he's got some explaining to do. Staying out all night better have been an emergency. If he would just hurry up and come home to explain, I'll be able to breathe again. Balancing the baby in one arm, I reach for his beeper with the other, unconsciously bouncing my knees to soothe my daughter's screams.

BEFORE

Andre. This man, I knew in my gut, was it. I finally understood what it meant, when "you just know." I just knew about Andre'. I met him at "The Loop" a trendy Burger restaurant not far from the apartment I shared with one of my sisters and we both worked.

I got a job at The Loop to make money while I was in nursing school. Having a restaurant job to pay the bills made me a cliché', but it was necessary and besides it gave the days structure.

On the first day of training at "The Loop," I sat with ten other new employees around a large, circular table, listening to Carl, the small, energetic, manager go over the corporate "steps of service." It was my second waitressing job – the first Famous Amos.," the only place that would hire me with no experience. That lasted two months. As Carl danced around the restaurant, demonstrating when to bring this and that to the table, I scanned the faces around the table, landing on dark brown eyes belonging to one of the three hires. He wasn't that tall, he had street swag and a great smile. Our eyes briefly locked, and he gave a quick and easy smile. I looked away, willing myself not to blush.

I learned long ago that the best way to survive in Jacksonville, Florida the **"Crab Capital"** of the state for black folks was to keep my defenses up at all times.

The meeting ended, and I gathered my notebook and pen and slid my sunglasses to rest on top of my head. I was almost through the doors leading to the streets before anyone else had even gotten up from the table I felt someone come up right behind me, and suddenly the door was opening. It was Andre', "Destiny, right?" Except for the way he said it, it sounded like "Wanna be with me?"

AFTER

Tina's screams fill my ears and penetrate the deep recesses of my brain where my decision-making neurons lie. My mind quick and sharp now feels vast and hollow. I have trouble thinking a single thought clearly. The beeper is still in my hand. My three-year-old daughter is still cradled in my arms. My brain jolted back into action as I read the message on the beeper. From that point, I knew he would have to come correct and answer questions I needed answers to. His all-night tryst was unacceptable. We needed to talk. His coming home after staying out all night seemed to be just a "G Thang" as he put it. I was tired of him treating me as if I had to accept his cheating. I wanted out. Enough was enough. I didn't know how I would make it with three children. But, I wasn't afraid to learn and that's all he needed to know.

This time I was leaving, and his overnight lovers would be surprised to know he no longer had a marriage curfew. I wasn't brand new to his game. I had become true to his game, knowing he would continue to play as long as I said or did nothing. My mind was made up. I was ending my participation and moving on with my three daughters. I deserved better and so did my babies. Little did I know how rejecting Andre; and not allowing him to have his way would create a rage I was unprepared to handle.

Ephesians 5:25
*Husbands, love **your** wives, just as Christ loved the church and gave himself up for her.*

Chapter 7

Destiny Divine Anthony – *former nurse, devoted wife, and loving mother of three daughters* was pronounced dead at 3:35 p.m. on May 12, 1987. On May 13, 1987, Dr. Flers for the Florida State medical examiners division performed an autopsy and declared the cause of Destiny's death as a shotgun wound to the head. It appeared that her death was tragically inevitable. But nothing, in this case, was as it seemed.

It would take many years and the unrelenting dedication of Destiny's middle daughter to solve the mystery of her death, unraveling a lifetime of dishonest deceit, searing betrayal, and an unfathomable cruel murder.

Andre Anthony led a life of contradictions. While he portrayed himself as a loving father and husband. With a marriage that had its ups and downs, it was **all a façade.**

Ephesians 5:28
In this same way, husbands ought to love their wives as their own bodies. He who loves his wife loves himself.

Chapter 8

Tatianna

Do you get over it? Do you ever get on with your life? Yes, I've gotten on with my life, but it is always a part of my life. And it does affect everything you do. Does it ever get easier to talk about her? No, it does not. But what amazes me now is how other people never wanted to talk to me about my mother. Did they think that we, meaning my sisters had forgotten her or hoped that we were too young to remember?

I could talk about other people I cared for who died years later, but subconsciously I suppressed any thought I had of my mother's death and tried to bury the pain. As I approached the age my mother was at the time of her death, I was acutely aware of my own mortality. Through the happy times, and through the difficult times, I am always painfully aware of not having her to share it with and the awful fact of never knowing her as an adult, only as a toddler. I would never be able to relate to her intellectually on an equal level or to say the least, as a growing child and daughter.

Being a mother, myself has been the most difficult and rewarding area in which the loss has affected me. The desire to remain the child in relationships, even parent-child, husband-wife can be a struggle to overcome and I love my children and husband to life!

I wonder how do I give a wealth of love when I sometimes feel empty in the place where a mother's love grows? How do I help my son and daughters feel good about their masculinity, femininity, sexuality, manhood, and womanhood when my mother died before I could learn these things from her?

As a motherless daughter, I needed answers. I had questions no one wanted to answer honestly or talk about. But as unnoticed as I was to others, God noticed me. God answered my prayers. How often do we get to revisit the past and revise the past? The Holy Spirit gave me that opportunity, as I earnestly in prayer sought him for the answers. Out of the three of us girls, the Holy Spirit allowed me to relive the day of my mother's murder as if I were there.

Some family members thought I was a little special. But what they did not know was this Un-Noticed/Special One; Tatianna had a gift that was formed in my mother's womb.

I started receiving visions of my mother's murder step by step. Whenever I would share the vision with family members, they would instantly remind me that I wasn't there, or I was too young to remember anything! Yet, the gift of prophecy was beginning to form in me as God began to reveal in the spirit the *answers I needed.*

Psalm 139:13
For you created my inmost being; you knit me together in my mother's womb.

Chapter 9

Gregory Drive in Jacksonville, Florida holds a special significance to me: It's where my mother was murdered. Jacksonville is where my sisters and I were born. It's also the place where two decades later I learned my background from the Holy Spirit after numerous lies from family members. The thoughts I have of Gregory Drive and Jacksonville transported me back to the pain and darkness my two sisters and I endured throughout our motherless childhoods with our profoundly troubled father.

My childhood in Jacksonville gave me a very personal awareness how people forced to take care of you can impact the lives of others. Growing up in Jacksonville my sisters and I faced extraordinary struggles that would have tested any child's strength and endurance. Somehow with God and determination, my siblings and I managed to find some comfort in each other.

My cast of resolute characters are my two sisters Tina the eldest and (Name) the baby girl. We were initially raised by our father's stepdad after our mother's murder. Our dad wasn't the fatherly type. He loved women, money, and the streets. Andre had more warrants out on him than he had kids and there are three of us.

His offenses? Where to start? He was wanted for driving without a license, driving with a suspended license, and bounced checks. Living with our father and step-granddaddy meant that my sisters and I wouldn't be separated.

Living at our step granddaddy's house led to injudicious actions from other adults and had disastrous consequences for my sisters and me. We were hurled into an emotional abyss.

Our daddy or step-granddaddy will never fully appreciate the lingering scars **Foster Care** left on us as children who ended up in the system.

As I began to write this book, trying to find the right words to express myself, a story took shape. At times the pain stabbed through my heart, plunging me into depression. I hated reliving those memories. But I had to seek and knock for the Holy Spirit to open the door of supernatural information.

Like most foster children, we had no choice of where we lived or how long we would stay. Others controlled our life.

According to "Lifting the Veil" research organization. A child in foster care is 28 times more likely to experience foster care sexual abuse, emotional deprivation and physical neglect.

Matthew 18:6 "If anyone causes one of these little ones—those who believe in me—to stumble, it would be better for them to have a large millstone hung around their neck and to be drowned in the depths of the sea.

Chapter 10

My sisters and I experienced our first sexual abuse at our step-granddaddy's home. When our step-granddaddy got mad it was nothing nice and this particular morning was one of those not nice mornings. My sisters and I had gotten up that morning and looked forward to what our Saturday would entail. We never knew. It could be a good Saturday, or it could be a not so good Saturday.

He started to shout out our names. I was dreading his tone alone. Sometimes when step-granddaddy got mad he would just yell and scream. But a lot of the time when our step-granddaddy got mad things went to the left really quick for my sisters and me!

"TATIANNA, TINA and TERRIE!" We jumped in fear. He stood in the kitchen holding a cigarette butt in the palm of his hand. "I found this in ya'll bed! Who's grown enough to be smoking?" We knew neither of us smoked. So, each of us denied knowing where the cigarette came from. Whether he knew or not, a man would come into our room every other night. He would fondle us and lay in the bed with us and no one knew it. As the Holy Spirit would bring back to my remembrance one of the men was a friend of our step-granddaddy's the other pedophile was our step-granddaddy's son.

On that morning granddaddy had this look. It was the same look people get when they have stepped in dog poop – a combination of disgust and anger.

In a rage, he said, "I'm gonna ask ya'll one more time. Where the hell did this cigarette, butt come from?" A knot grew in my stomach. I remember the men coming into our room, climbing into our beds. They would touch each of us in an inappropriate manner. What could we say and who could we tell? We were too young to convey how each one of these disgusting men was guilty. Our step-granddaddy's son would often stay some nights. Both were dirty, filthy men. We were afraid to speak for fear of a whipping. He would never believe a word we said. We were already children of the system. **Foster Care** children. Children forced to be taken care of by those who only wanted a check but not the children.

He stormed out of the kitchen in anger. I knew he was going to get his belt. We heard his voice become louder through the closed kitchen door like an angry fist blocked by a pillow. For several minutes he was silent and within seconds . . . "Answer me!" he shouted. The three of us started to cry. "I'm going to have to teach ya'll a lesson." He was about to walk back out and then he stopped completely, standing apparently distracted by his thoughts, he looked at me and pointed in my direction. "Get up and go in the front room and sit your ass in a chair!" I did as I was told. I didn't want to get a whipping. I sat in silence. I knew I would be called a liar if I said anything.

Granddaddy walked back into the kitchen and placed a tea kettle filled with water on the stove to boil. As the water boiled he went to the back porch and returned with a large yellow foot tub. While he did this, a knock at the front door interrupted him. He looked through the peephole.

Granddaddy looked at me and said in an irritated tone, "Don't say a word." A member of his church stopped by to visit. He greeted the church member asked them to come in and have a seat. He excused himself from the church member.

He came into the area where I sat and poured the boiling water into the foot tub which was placed in front of me. He added a touch of cold water. Between clenched teeth, he said, "Put your feet in the water. You better not open your mouth!" The water was scalding hot. I flinched in pain as tears ran down my little cheeks. I moaned as quietly as I could. A scream was waiting to be released and I knew more pain would come if released. I placed my hands over my mouth.

Granddaddy went back to where his church member sat and had a short conversation with him before he explained he was sorry he couldn't sit and talk long. He needed to see about his granddaughters who had been "cutting up."

I heard granddaddy say, "I'll see you on Sunday." He shut the front door and came into the room and stood in front of me. He handed me a pack of cigarettes and said, "Since you want to smoke, you can smoke this whole pack of cigarettes with me and my friends." I cried from both pain and fear. Between agony and defeat I tried to talk, "Granddaddy, I didn't smoke no cigarettes. I don't know where the butt came from." He did not believe me and said, "I'm going to make you remember where the cigarette butt came from and you will never in life want to smoke again!"

I can't explain the hurt, the pain, the agony and humiliation I felt as an innocent, unloved child. I wished I had my momma, a wish that crossed my mind constantly. Especially when I was being punished by granddaddy.

He took a box of matches from his pocket and snatched the pack of cigarettes from me. He placed a cigarette to his mouth and lit it. He inhaled and exhaled, then handed it to me. "Smoke it!" he shouted and pushed the cigarette to my lips. Every time I took a puff I would gag, choke and cough. I can recall puffing on four cigarettes. Because he held four cigarette butts in his hand afterward. Through my tears and coughing, he said, "You ain't gonna want to smoke again!"

<u>2 Corinthians 6:14</u> *Do not be unequally yoked with unbelievers. For what partnership has righteousness with lawlessness? Or what fellowship has light with darkness?*

Chapter 11

I was finally allowed to take my feet from the foot tub and return to our bedroom. I went to my room and cried so much my sisters cried with me. He always made my sisters sit in the kitchen and listen to him punish me when he wasn't punishing all three of us at the same time. I was a bit rebellious. I was so mad because of my punishment I threatened to burn the house down. I did not understand how powerful my thoughts were. I didn't understand that the power of our thoughts was where many strongholds began.

On this particular day, my sisters and I sat in the family den where we placed papers in a boxed fan. The papers caught on fire engulfing the den in flames. Our step-grandmother rushed the three of us to the hospital emergency room.

Once we were discharged and arrived home, we received whippings from our step-granddaddy. He never failed to use a belt to lash on our legs.

My sisters and I were very young when we were physically, mentally, and sexually abused by our step-granddaddy's friend and son. It took us a while before we decided to tell anyone what we'd been through. I was scared about what had happened and didn't know who to turn to.

Looking back, it feels like I lost my childhood. As I grew older, I had problems sleeping with night terrors. I used to find it difficult to concentrate in school and had problems remembering stuff.

After the fire incident, things got worse, the abuse, the punishments, the men coming into our room at night. I decided it had to stop. We went to school and I asked my teacher if I could talk to her. She was always asking us questions. "How are you? Are you alright? Where did that bruise come from on your arm?"

She was very concerned and observed all of her students. She was a nice teacher and I liked her. Even at that, I was still scared and worried that she might not believe me.

Once I shared our dilemma, my teacher and counselor were on top of the information immediately. They assured us we would not be hurt anymore and contacted **Child Protective Services.**

Child Protective Services contacted our legal aunts. Our aunts had a hard time convincing the courts of the abuse. Our step-granddaddy was cunning and had members of his church to vouch for him being a true Christian and good person who wouldn't hurt a soul. They told of all the good deeds he performed in the church. The system believed the hype and we found ourselves back in harm's way until our aunts decided to kidnap us.

Matthew 18:6
But whoso shall offend one of these little ones which believe in me, it were better for him that a millstone were hanged about his neck, and that he were drowned in the depth of the sea.

Chapter 12

Our kidnapping took place just as we were about to get on the school bus to go home. We were approached by one of our aunts. My mother's sister. She said, "Hey girls, you're not going back to that hell hole. I'm taking you to Baltimore to live with another one of mine and your mom's sister." We asked no questions and piled into the back seat of her car. We drove to the airport and it seemed in minutes we were walking through the automatic doors. We had no luggage or clothes, we had what we wore to school that day and that was it!

Our hearts pounded as the three of us followed our aunt and walked through the doors of the Jacksonville airport. We didn't care. All we understood was, we were not going back to our step-granddaddy's house!

We entered the airport for the first time. Our fears were overwhelming as we got closer and closer to the ticket area. We were now about to board a plane to Baltimore, Maryland. Our first plane ride to where one of our mother's sister lived.

My sisters and I were squeezing each other's hands as our aunt held my hand and quickly walked us to the ticket counter. We were told to stand to the side close to our aunt. She walked up to the counter to get our tickets. I was thankful to have our aunt with us because she helped us to stay calm. We sat down to wait for the boarding call. Then I heard it "flight 375 to Baltimore, Maryland is now boarding." After our aunt handed a pretty flight attendant, our tickets we got on the plane.

The flight attendant, who was wearing a blue dress with a red bow, said, "Welcome aboard flight 375 to Baltimore." My sisters and I were all seated together. Our aunt was in the same row across from us seated in the first seat. The engines roared as I got more and more scared. The plane started to move down the runway. My hands started to shake as the plane got faster and faster down the runway. So then finally we were in the air and that's when I calmed down. One hour and fifty minutes later we were on the ground. Even though I was nervous I still got through it.

We were excited but a little nervous to be moving to a new place and out of town! We had to get used to another house. New schools, and a new relative.

There was never a time in my life that I wasn't lonely or afraid. Even as a toddler I knew I was different, the odd one out. The reason for all the conflict in our family. I knew because I was told every single day by our step-granddaddy. "You're rebellious, you don't mind nobody!"

Anything that got broken or went wrong, was my fault. I welcomed a fresh start. Because every day our granddaddy told me I was getting on his nerves, making him sick. His life would have been better if I had never been born. My sisters were blameless, but I was the troublemaker.

When you're told often enough that you are worthless, stupid, a liar you believe it's true! What was wrong with me? Why was I so bad and unloved? I was only a little girl. Trying hard to fit in. But when you think you're worthless you don't stand up for yourself. I was imbalanced. I felt worthless, but I also rebelled! So, when an evil person or a bad person is around you're really in trouble. There's no one to turn to and nowhere you'll be safe. I had to fight for me and my sisters. Evil people target the vulnerable they can sniff them out.

Right through our early childhood my sisters and I were never protected. Never safe. Most children run to their mother when they are scared and unhappy or when something unspeakable happens to them. For me and my sisters that was never going to work. We were unwanted. Unloved. Completely alone.

Psalm 10:7 "Their mouths are full of cursing and hate."

The Un-Noticed

Chapter 13

Moving to Baltimore appeared to be a new beginning. We would be loved. We would be wanted. And for me, I would be **noticed.**

But I had a keen sense of lies. Our granddaddy helped me with that. As a child my sisters and I expected this new move to be better. Much better. I mean we were with our mother's blood sister, our aunt. How could she not treat us like her own? How could she not understand her three young nieces feeling unwanted and afraid? Wanting only to be safe and loved after losing their mother? Her sister!

We finally arrived at our aunt's home. Aunt Harriet, the aunt we called mom when she allowed us to. Some days she preferred us to call her **Hattie or Harriet.** We wanted to call her momma. Connecting to someone who we believed loved and wanted us like their own meant having a momma. She tried in her own way to explain that our momma was deceased, and she wasn't our real mother. I guess that was the reason she didn't want us to call her momma.

As we settled into our new location, the transitions took place quickly. All efforts to stop our daddy from finding us were in place. We were not traceable. We had new names and birth certificates to match. All illegal. An appointment with a doctor was made. Shot records would be needed in order to enroll us in school. We enrolled in school and afterward, Aunt Yvonne took us shopping for school clothes. That made us happy. We had a fresh start.

Aunt Yvonne received a check from the government to help provide for us.

During that time, we were never hungry. Provisions were made for us. We were clean and very well taken care of in appearance.

Unfortunately, Aunt Yvonne never had children of her own. Which made it difficult for her to be a loving aunt or mother figure to me and my sisters. It eventually came to light she had no idea what to expect when it came to raising children. Let alone, three small girls.

We expected her to know how to raise us. We expected this new home to be different. We were not prepared to leave one abusive home only to relocated to another. Here's what I kept thinking in my childish mind and we were finally settled into our new home in Baltimore. *"None of this would have happened if our momma wasn't dead. We wouldn't be living with our mother's sister who really didn't love us."* My sisters and I were very disappointed we expected getting away from our step-granddaddy was like a dream come true, ----but it wasn't to be.

We thought we were safe knowing aunt Harriet was never married. She was single. Nevertheless, she had her choice of male friends. The fact that our aunt's boyfriends were cheaters and liars didn't surprise me. One of them had tried me and my sisters. My aunt didn't play the radio. She would kick them to the curb quick. She'd say she could find another man in a heartbeat and she would always make good on her promise and find someone else new. Her boyfriend Kenny was one of those finders.

Ecclesiastics 3: 17 - "I said to myself, in due season God will judge everyone, both good and bad, for all their deeds."

Chapter 14

With every cruel degrading word our aunt spoke to us; with every single whipping she gave to me or my sisters, killed our confidence and self-esteem slowly. She was destroying us from the inside out. She stole our innocence and once again took away all sense of safety and stability. She conditioned us to fear everything and trust no one. Surviving her forced me to build walls. Everything I would become both intentionally and unintentionally, both good and bad, stemmed directly from the abuse my sisters and I suffered at the hands of our Aunt Yvonne for years. And being helpless to stop it was an unfathomable torment.

The earliest memory of abuse from our aunt I have is from when I was about four or five years old. There were times when my sisters and I would play and make too much noise. Aunt Yvonne would yell at us. "What the hell is all that noise for?! Ya'll need to shut the hell up. I'm trying to rest! Ya'll so damn stupid. Ya'll little worthless asses need to be quiet. I don't know why the hell I adopted ya'll!" Me and my sisters would hold on to each other and cry. We were scared to death a whipping would be next. What was happening? We really didn't mean to wake her up. We couldn't help but cry. I would try to be brave and explain. "We were just playing, we didn't mean to wake you up momma." My aunt picked up a lamp on the nightstand and threw it at us. It missed, but shattered to pieces against the wall behind us, she yelled, "I don't give a s*** what you *were* doing, I want it quiet in this damn house!" Our aunt said what she meant and meant exactly what she said. She slammed the door closed, and a few seconds later, we heard her bedroom door slam shut.

Even though I was the middle child, I always wanted to protect my sisters. We huddled together as I held them close to me. Even at my young age, there was an inner strength inside of me that refused to break. My sisters needed me, and I needed them.

Neither of us spoke a word. We were too afraid. My baby sister concentrated so hard on trying not to cry out loud she began to hyperventilate. I rocked her back and forth gently patting her back until she calmed down. It had to be God to give me the instinct and strength to hold us up through the pain and abuse.

We lay down together and snuggled up as tightly as we could. I laid there in my sister's arms for what seemed like forever before fading off to sleep.

I awoke in the middle of the night and picked up the shattered pieces of the lamp. I placed them in the small trash can in our room. I feared we would be whipped if it wasn't cleaned up when our aunt woke us up for school the next morning.

Why was our aunt so mean to us? We didn't have a choice in relocating to Baltimore. I didn't want to cry. Why didn't she care about us like an aunt should? Why didn't she care that me and my sisters were hurting? Why had she said such mean things to us? I didn't know the answers to any of these questions, but the heaviness of the whole thing really hurt my little heart.

All morning I could hardly keep the tears at bay. Even at school, as much as I needed to pay attention to my teacher, I thought only about what had happened at home and how scared I was. And sad. It hurt to think that my momma's sister didn't care about us and was so angry at us for being little girls laughing and playing in our room. And as much as those things hurt me and my sisters it hurt more thinking about the mean things she said to us. What is a five- year old to do with that? I mean, how do you put it in place, and move past it? I just didn't know. The incident birthed anxiety into my young life and it would become my constant companion.

Ecclesiastic 4:1 Again, I observed all the oppression that takes place under the sun. I saw the tears of the oppressed, with no one to comfort them. The oppressors have great power, and their victims are helpless.

The Un-Noticed

Chapter 15

We never laughed out loud in our room after that. We giggled and whispered at whatever was funny to us. Especially when we realized our aunt was asleep or napping and we were awake.

I couldn't have known at the age of five that the abuse would become much more frequent and far worse in nature. It was a progression, by the age of seven, I was sure eventually would end in death. I think it's hard for people who have never experienced child abuse, how it can go on for so long, how it has the chance to escalate to such terrifying heights. But that's the thing about child abuse, it's a silent killer. Child abuse lives in the darkness where its secrets grow roots. And everyone involved is ruled by fear, under the full control of their abuser and the only way to survive is to keep it a secret from others and the world. Others and a world that wouldn't believe them. In most cases of child abuse, there is an unspoken but definite understanding between abuser and victim: you get to live in exchange for silence. Th real problem with that understanding is that when the abuser decides to revoke it, the victim doesn't see it coming.

My aunt's boyfriend Kenny would place a pillow over our face and lay on top of it until he felt we were about to die. A game he played after he had touched us inappropriately. He always knew how much time it took before we would stop breathing. I fought with every inch of my body which was no match for a grown man. He'd get up and laugh like it was the funniest thing. These sick games frightened me and my sisters.

I never knew from day to day if my sisters and I were going to die at the hands of our aunt's boyfriend Kenny, or her physical abuse as well. Neither of us believed that either of them was not capable of ending our lives.

Despite our disappointment at home, we welcomed going to school. I made friends easily. I worked hard at getting people to like me. The school was an outlet for freedom. Baltimore was another pit stop. No long-term home life for me and my sisters. We were told, Jacksonville, Florida would take us back. From pillar to post. We had no way of knowing how to hold up the post we were destined to be underneath.

Ecclesiastics 4:12 "A person standing alone can be attacked and defeated, but two can stand back-to-back and conquer. Three are even better, for a triple-braided cord is not easily broken."

Chapter 16

Our return to Jacksonville, Florida proved to be detrimental to my sisters and I. Most little girls have hugs and love. They are told they are pretty and princesses. They are treasured. All the love they need, they are given by the person whose love they should have by rights - their mother. But my sisters and I would never be fortunate to receive that right. Instead, we would be dealt a losing hand that only God could turn into a winning hand.

We took to living in Jacksonville like stray cats that never knew real meals until someone took it home. Which was how we learned to be independent. We learned to cook our own food when there was food for us to eat.

Our return to Jacksonville in July began with moving into an apartment we would occupy for one month. We moved in with one of Aunt Yvonne's friend. We moved from every place we thought we would call home. Anxiety and hopelessness filled me and my sister's lives. Which led to an emotional rollercoaster of living wherever the wind blew us.

Any time we settled into an apartment with our aunt after moving back to Jacksonville we were told to gather our things and get ready for yet another move.

By the middle of November, we had changed schools three times and had a new apartment addresses every four months. The last apartment number I remember was #338. The frequent school changes, left huge gaps in our academic and social development. At a time when other children were having slumber parties, playing sports, engaging in school activities, we were worried about where we would sleep that night.

1 Timothy 5:8 Anyone who does not provide for their relatives, and especially for their own household, has denied the faith and is worse than an unbeliever.

The Un-Noticed

Chapter 17

School was a safe haven for me. But some days I wished I didn't have to attend. I was either too tired from a lack of sleep, too hungry from a lack of food or both. My teacher noticed right away that I was far behind academically. I also fell asleep in class quite often. My teacher would write notes to my aunt (that I would never give to her for fear of a whipping) and even worked with me in a small group, hoping for improvement.

One day my teacher questioned me because I could not read the story I had been assigned for homework. She was very firm and told me I needed to do her homework if I was going to see good results. I started crying and, in our conversation, I blurted out that we were staying with our aunt and cousins. I told her there was no electricity. There were not enough beds, so my sisters and I slept on a tiny sofa together. I told her that rats ran along the back of the couch at night and I could not sleep because I was so scared.

My teacher scheduled a conference with our Aunt Yvonne and she confirmed that we were waiting to be placed in an apartment through section 8 and she worked nights and we were going through bad times. My aunt cried and cried like she felt so bad that she wasn't helping us. I was sent back to P.E. and my teacher talked to my aunt.

When my sisters and I got home from school, the wrath of Aunt Yvonne was in full effect. "Tatianna, I know damn well you didn't have me go to that school and try to keep the authorities off of me because of your big ass mouth? So, you snitching on me? Huh?" I knew what was coming next and my body tensed up.

Just as my head lifted a bit, I caught the image of her hand coming towards me. Then a big slap in my face came down hard, I fell to the side, my balance off. The left side of my face stinging but yet not as harsh as the sound made as the hand connected with my cheek. Her voice stumbling with a harsh tone, interjecting with pure enjoyment, "Do not look at me like you gonna do something crazy. DO NOT LOOK AT ME!" Her voice rang like the school bell in the afternoon.

"You better keep your mouth shut from now on or I'll beat the living crap out of you! Do you understand Tatianna?" I nodded. But I knew in my heart I wanted to hurt her back and I would. My two sisters, watched, too astonished to move.

"And all three of ya'll better pull your damn grades up. You got retained in Baltimore. You don't need to get retained no more!" She looked at us with pure contempt. She had the nerve to say, "I ain't raising three damn dummies. Not on my watch!" As if she helped us do homework or took us to the library. Over the years, Aunt Yvonne kicked and beat us, threw us down the stairs and pushed us into a scalding hot bath. She once held my head under water and another time she shoved a full bar of soap in my mouth. There are too many incidents to recount.

2 Samuel 13:14
But he refused to listen to her, and since he was stronger than she, he raped her.

Chapter 18

The fist beatings and emotional abuse continued. I wanted out! I was afraid and tired I would take a stapler and use it to staple my head, in school just to get attention. My sisters and I didn't have a way of escape in the natural, but God knew what we needed.

My bruises were very bad, they drew attention from yet another teacher. I was escorted to the office and the guidance counselor questioned me and my sisters individually. They figured if we all lived together each of us was being abused. Not just one of us.

My sisters were as tired of the abuse as I was, and we sang like the fat lady! We shared how our Aunt Yvonne's *newest* live-in boyfriend Stanley would do drugs, get high and drunk in our presence and force us to smoke weed or drink alcohol and touch us inappropriately.

Stanley and Aunt Yvonne would fight like heavyweight champions. Stanley would always win. He would knock her out and leave her for dead. We would always clean her up and get her in bed to rest. Stanley would steal her car at least three times a week. She couldn't go to work, and we would have to walk about five miles to school because she didn't give us money for a bus pass. She didn't want us on the school bus because we would fight all the time from being picked on by other children.

Aunt Yvonne would kick Stanley out and he would burst the windows in her bedroom and threaten to kill her while he was beating the living daylights out of her. By the grace of God, she was able to remove herself as well as my sisters and me away from Stanley.

When the Department of Children and Families visited the home, they found that there was no food or electricity. The water and electricity had been off for close to three weeks. When questioned, she said she was unable to get to work because her car wasn't drivable, and the lights would be on the next day. She showed them the date she got her stamps which would be in two days. Aunt Yvonne told them a relative was taking her to the **Food Bank** that day to get some food. They just hadn't gotten there to pick her up yet. DCF investigators took notes and we were taken to a hotel for temporary shelter until everything we needed to live normal was in place.

After that incident with DCF. Aunt Yvonne seemed to take a tad more interest in us by teaching us how to become independent. We learned how to do laundry, cook easy meals and catch the city bus. We were between the ages of 8-10 years old.

We were able to focus on our school work. Only because we helped each other and did our best. Aunt Yvonne worked long hours at night. We were left alone to fend for ourselves. At least we didn't have to worry about Stanley anymore. Aunt Yvonne wouldn't bring a man into the house to stay after the abuse from Stanley. However, she never really acknowledged the abuse. She simply swept the issue away like unwanted trash placed in the garbage. Never to be thought of again.

There were times my sisters and I would provide the support and nurture that was not consistently provided by our Aunt Yvonne. We served as a buffer against the worst effects of harsh circumstances. And then things changed.

Sibling rivalry reared its head in my relationship with my sisters around the time we relocated back to Jacksonville. The rivalry was not healthy. We competed with each other and showed animosity toward each other. We were abusive toward each other verbally. Meaning we would curse each other out like grown-ups.

During this time, we fought and competed with each other for time, attention, toys, food and a host of other things. We spent almost every waking moment with each other than with anyone else growing up. I guess this behavior was to be a given due to the circumstances and the environment we were forced to embrace.

My sisters and I were home alone most of the time. We made our dinner, prepared for school and put ourselves to bed. We were three little girls with grown-up responsibilities. Those responsibilities had each one of us acting like we were grown enough to say and do what we wanted when there was no adult supervision.

Chapter 19

Sweetwater was where our summers started. You could smell the bar-b-que from neighboring backyards. We'd hear the loud music playing in the backyards of neighbors chilling out and eating their favorite seafood; crabs and the fixings, potatoes, corn, neckbones, Rodger Woods sausages and boiled eggs.

Sweetwater was a community on the West side of Jacksonville, Florida. Where many African American families called home. Firestone road, Wilson Boulevard those street s rang home for many.

Our grandmother and grandfather lived in Sweetwater. There were two other relatives living in our grandparent's home. Grandma's handicapped uncle and her son.

Aunt Yvonne would ship us off to spend a summer we definitely would not be willing to write an essay on **"How did you spend your summer?"** when we returned to school in the fall. I mean seriously, a teacher with a creative writing degree would probably have given us an "A." But a teacher seeking correct grammar, punctuation, and a normal summer vacation essay would direct our papers to the principal's office. Because they would be ***raw, ratchet and real.***

Stories unbelievable to the eyes of the reader coming from an eleven-year-old writer.

There would be no baking cookies and brownies at our grandma's house. We didn't take bubble baths and look at the television before being tucked into bed. There was no night time "Our Father prayers."

Our mornings were early. We woke up only to have a list of chores to do. Cutting the grass. Cleaning our grandma's house and any chores she and the other adults in the house could find for us to do while they got drunk.

Oh, and getting drunk was a given. The house was filled with our grandparent's and uncle's friends getting drunk throughout the entire day.

We'd left the comforts of a home that had running water to take our baths. At grandma's house, they boiled water and used a foot tub to bathe in! Three to four days would pass before we were able to take a bath.

We went dumpster diving for cans and food like an athlete executing a dive in the Olympic competitions hoping to win the Gold medal. We hoped for a little less than a Gold medal. We hoped for food and a visit to the corner store afterward.

Proverbs 22:6
Start children off on the way they should go, and even when they are old they will not turn from it.

The Un-Noticed

Chapter 20

Living with alcoholics sucked, even worse than being around alcoholics was being abused by them. What would child molestation look like through the eyes of the children being abused? This was NOT a fairy tale!

Our handicapped uncle had a field day molesting us. He found the perfect opportunity when no one was around, or when they would gather under the *hang-out tree*. The hang-out tree was where they would all go hang out and get drunk, play cards, talk smack and have fun. But the most opportunistic time to molest us was when everyone was asleep. He would come into our room and start fingering us and from there penetration. No one ever knew, and we were in no position to fight back or tell.

He would make us walk to the corner store with him where he'd purchase cigarettes and beer. But for us, he'd buy candy and chips. His sadistic behavior favored molesting us on the church grounds. Our grandma's backyard was also a place he enjoyed raping us and his favorite place was in the room next to our grandparents.

It started off in the usual way: everyone asleep. Me in bed, my sisters sleeping, the voice at the door. I did what I was told and performed the sex act. I would think it was over and he would open my legs -- he started to touch me, I didn't like it and asked him to stop. But he wouldn't he told me to shut up and placed his hand over my mouth. I saw fire in his eyes and I was terrified. The next thing I knew his big heavy body was on top of me, tears streamed down my face from the pain and fear and shock of what was happening. He kept pushing until I thought I was going to split in two, I thought I was going to die my face set with tears, but I didn't make a sound. I lay there in terrible pain frozen with shock. My whole body, my head, my heart all felt broken. When he finished, he told me to go to bed.

The next day I was very sore and noticed I had a handprint on my little leg and bruised inside my thighs. I wanted to tell my grandma. I wanted to scream so loudly how much I was hurting, I wanted to show her the marks on me. I wanted to cry in her arms and be held by her, but I knew she wouldn't believe me and if I told her she wound blame me and I would get in so much trouble. I was only seven years old.

We carried this secret afraid, angry, frustrated, and full of hate towards those who were supposed to protect us and would not. We watched each other go through these horrible acts of abuse mentally and physically. Forced to pretend our lives were normal. When we never knew what normal looked like. We only felt that what we were experiencing was definitely not normal!

The memories have haunted us to this day. We suffered in silence from an innocence stolen. We lived in disparity each and every day during our summers at grandma's house. I personally never thought as a child the chains that bound my soul could not be broken.

Time moved on. As young girls, we were coming of age. There would be no *bar mitzvah*, or *sweet* whatever age party for us. We were at the age (I was 11) where boys interest us. Guess who had to be placed on birth control? Me, Tatianna, the **Unnoticed One.** I had started my menstrual cycle and was accused by our mother (Aunt Yvonne) of having sex because I started my menstrual cycle at an early age. Needless to say, I was not sexually active willingly. I had been raped!

Psalm 147: 3
He heals the brokenhearted and binds up their wounds.

Chapter 21

Out of the blue at the age of eleven-years-old I had become the caretaker of my godbrother, Chris. I was in the sixth grade! Why I was **chosen,** I had no idea. I wasn't even the oldest child. Our mother decided to take him in. His mother had been on crack and I guess our mother felt she was being a **Shero**. Only to pass him off to me.

On this particular morning, I awoke to Chris's screams. I looked up and saw my little godbrother crying his eyes out. "What wrong Chris?" I'd asked, sitting up quickly. "T.T. I'm hungry." I got up off the bed. I made my way to the kitchen with Chris trailing behind me. I was responsible for getting Chris dressed and ready for school. I found cereal in the pantry and grabbed milk from the refrigerator and retrieved a bowl from the cabinet. I fixed Chris cereal and watched him gulp it down like he had never eaten. I ate what was left. "Come on Chris, let's get you dressed for school." I had his clothes laying on the dresser the night before. We went into the tiny bathroom and I washed his face, made him brush his teeth and combed his hair. "Ouch T.T." Chris wiggled away from me. "You can't go to school with a nappy head. You're too cute to look ugly." His face beamed like a light bulb when he smiled, and I gave him a hug. "Go sit on the bed and watch cartoons until I get dressed." He did what he was told.

Afterward, I washed up and brushed my teeth, I put on a pair of jeans and a top and pulled my hair back into a ponytail. I only had fifty cents to make an emergency phone call if I needed to. It was Friday and I'd have to catch the bus to get Chris from school after I got out of school. The issue was, catching the bus from the Westside of town to the Southside of town and then back to the Westside. The distance was quite a way for an eleven-year-old alone with a five- year old. I did as I was told.

I got Chris on the school bus and waved goodbye. He seemed happy, knowing someone was there for him. I wondered how God could place someone in my life to care for when no one in my life cared for me.

I finally got on my school bus all the while hating I had to go to school at all. Deep down inside I had a strong desire to help Chris learn his ABC's and learn to read. In a way, it helped me to understand how important an education was. Some things I realize happened because God was simply preparing me. There is always PAIN IN GROWTH. I didn't realize it as an eleven-year-old then, but God knew. It just didn't seem fair that an eleven-year old should have the responsibility of taking care of a five-year-old. I learned quickly that life was not fair at all!

Chapter 22

"Tatianna, Tatianna! Bring your ass in here!" I was immune to the screams, the beatings, and the name calling. I would mimic every word she said to me as I walked into her bedroom. So, I took my time walking to her room and let her ass scream. Maybe she'd develop strep throat. Then I wouldn't have to hear her voice at all.

I stood at the door entrance of her bedroom. "Girl, what in the hell is this?" She waved a piece of paper around in her hand as if I could read what was on it. I shrugged and didn't say a word. "Oh, so now your ass can't talk?" She jumped up from the bed and lunged for me. I sidestepped her ass and she fell to the floor. "I'ma whip your ass for that!" She struggled to get up from the floor and once she got her balance she grabbed me by the arm and pushed me toward the bed. Mom (Aunt Yvonne) reached for a thick, wide, black, leather, belt. The belt she *always* had hanging on the doorknob, waiting to swing on me or my sisters the way a tennis racket swung at a tennis ball. She started swinging it across my body as she talked and whipped. "Why (swish!) … is (swish!) … you (swish!) … got (swish!) … all (swish!) these (swish!) … Fefefefefef's (swish!) . . . on your report card?" It seemed like she loved the sound of the letter "*F*" so…. much she couldn't let it go! "You wanna be a dummy all your damn life? You can screw boys and shit, but you can't read and write? You ain't gonna be stupid around here for long. I'ma put your ass out if you don't get it together Tatianna!" I pressed my face closer into the mattress, and let the tears sink onto the bedspread and prayed she'd soon stop swinging that belt. Thank God she allowed me to keep on my clothes. It didn't hurt so bad.

My thoughts were jumbled with how could she, and why would she? Didn't she understand that raising a child was a job? Oh, I forgot, she couldn't know because she never raised anything. Not even a plant. I could barely sleep through the night. Chris had nightmares and I'm sure he had these symptoms from being diagnosed a crack baby. I'm eleven and knew that! Why didn't my mom (Aunt Yvonne) know that? My grades were bad way before she got the report card. She obviously didn't think about looking at the PROGRESS REPORT! That report alone told you exactly what your child was doing in school or what subjects they needed to improve or not.

The plot thickens and "Here Comes the Bride." No one was really invited. It just happened. ***"I's married now!"*** Our mom (Aunt Yvonne) smiled like **Sophia** in the movie ***The Color Purple*** when she finally married a man named Willie. Happiness was short lived in that marriage. Willie was abusive on drugs and an alcoholic. The same old pattern in her men. She had a history of loving men with those type of characteristics.

We visited our grandmother one weekend and all hell broke loose. We had gotten into the car to leave and Willie was mad. He called our mom everything but the child of God. "You piece of crap. When I get my hands on you I'm gonna kill your ass.!" She tried to ignore him while she sat in the front seat of the car. At least she thought silence would be golden, but not for Willie. He backhanded her right in front of us. **WHAM!** He struck her as hard as he could. She immediately embraced her left eye. He didn't hesitate to take his fist and punch **WHAM!** Another blow to the right eye. She tried to shield her face from him hitting her again, but he repeatedly landed blows to whatever place his fist found open prey. With one hand on the steering wheel. She crumpled over when he did the unthinkable and hit her in the back of her head with his right fist. This time she coughed up blood.

My sister Tina started hitting him in the back of his head while we were in the back seat "Stop hitting our momma!" She screamed and kept hitting his head with her small fist. He tried to cover his head and drive at the same time. "Ya'll better sit ya'll asses down back there are I'll kill all of us in this damn car." We could tell he was in pain. I screamed. "Momma, momma!" She could barely move. We started throwing blows upside his head. And Tina went for the jugular and bit him on the back of his neck breaking skin. He howled like a wounded animal. I don't know if it was the pain or the distraction that had him almost run head-on into another car. He swerved over into the right lane and pulled over onto the side of the road. He put the car in park and jumped out of the vehicle. He held on to the back of his neck as blood poured through his fingers.

"Coward, punk, drunk, "I called him every name I could. Momma was coming to and she slid over in the driver's seat still in pain. When I saw her regain her strength to get home, I should have known those same genes were built in me. Those genes that defied the odds of abuse and neglect.

Her eyes were so swollen she could barely see to drive. Momma/Aunt Yvonne was almost unrecognizable. We said nothing all the way home. We were glad to be alive. Praying Willie's ass wouldn't come back. That prayer was not answered that day!

Chapter 23

Somehow, we made it home safe and sound. Momma was beaten up pretty bad. Her eyes had swollen shut. She gave us instructions to help the swelling to go down. We placed ice in two sandwich bags and wrapped the bags in two separate washcloths to place over both of her eyes. She took a *Goody* to stop her headache and laid down until the next morning.

We, of course, had to fix our own dinner. Hot dogs and beans. We were as exhausted as our momma. Tina was so proud of biting the mess out of Willie's neck. "I bit him so hard, his skin came off." She said proudly. "Well, you better gargle your throat and mouth with some *Listerine* because he might have some kind of disease!" Terrie, the baby girl said. We laughed so hard talking about Willie. "I bet his head is hurting so bad he's probably somewhere drunk or at the Emergency Room!" I said, laughing. "T.T. you kept pounding on his head, his ear, and where ever your fist landed!" Tina said shaking her head.

"Yeah, I didn't care if he ran into another car and killed us all. I felt at least we would never have to go through the hell we've been through again. Heaven would be better." We got quiet. Nothing else was said. I showered, and Tina took a bath and Terrie followed. We slept away the pain. I dreamed I was in Heaven.

It was only a dream. I awoke to Willie's voice. "Why can't you call your job and tell them *your* daughter is sick? She ain't nunna my child!" My mom was really afraid of him. She calmly reminded him, "I don't have any leave time left to take off. I won't get paid if I do and we need the money." Mom was a Dietician. She worked at a Nursing Home.

My oldest sister Tina needed to go to the Emergency Room. Tina had a sore throat and it pained her to speak. Willie snatched the keys off the table. "Come on ya'll. Let's go." He started walking toward the door. "You gonna be late for work if you don't come on now!" He looked at my sister Tina who needed him to take her to the ER and said, "I ain't gonna be at no doctor's office all damn day!"

Chapter 24

On this day the weather was clear, blue skies, no clouds, spring was in the air. I sat in my room with the windows up. I was prepared for my weekend visit with my favorite uncle. I could relax and take my time. I was home alone. Mom was at work, Tina and Willie went to the ER and Terrie had an afterschool event.

The fun part was picking out what to wear while I was at my uncles for the weekend. I got the iron and picked out my favorite bell bottom pants to iron. I had my room door closed. It was simply a habit. I was excited and preoccupied about the weekend. I was startled when I heard a knock at my bedroom door. I didn't answer. "Hey Tatianna, you in there?" It was Willie. He knocked again. I still didn't answer. He cracked the door open, peered around the room. He asked, "Are you ok?" I nodded and said, "Where's Tina?" He walked into the room and said, "She's at the ER. They were taking too long. I told her to call me when she was ready to come home." He sat down next to me on the floor where I was ironing my pants. "You wanna go to the store with me? I got some money."

My hands trembled, and the iron fell over. I fumbled trying to get up from the floor. I could feel my heart pounding. I stuttered, "No, no, I don't." It appeared he was getting up to leave, instead he said, "OK" and he locked the door, cutting off the escape route for me. If I did scream, the screams that would come behind my bedroom door would not attract any attention in the empty house.

He walked toward me, and as he got closer he began to grope my breast with his hands. "Don't do that! You're not supposed to be in my room! Get your hands off of me! I'm going to tell." He smirked, his breath reeked of alcohol. "Who you gonna tell? Ain't nobody gonna believe you!"

He pushed me down on the carpet and stripped my shorts off and inserted his fingers between my legs. While he felt satisfaction, I felt violated, humiliated and defenseless. He was biting his bottom lip to keep from moaning out in pleasure. "Please stop. Get off of me!" I cried uncontrollably. He heard a door close. He jumped up off of me, "Put your shorts on and go wipe your face and don't tell nobody!" He walked away,

I put on my shorts and ran as fast as I could out of my room through the house. Seeing if my mom had come in. When I didn't see anyone, I ran out of the house to a neighbor's house. I tried to call my mom from the neighbor's phone, but I wasn't able to reach her.

So, I called my uncle that I planned to visit for the weekend. The phone rang once, and he immediately answered. I was stuttering with my words and cried at the same time. "T, slow down. What's wrong?" He asked. I could barely talk and said, "Willie tried to rape me. He came into my room while I was home by myself. He drove Tina to the ER because her throat was hurting, and momma couldn't take off from work." I paused to catch my breath. "He left her at the ER and came back to the house. Willie came into my room and started touching me!" My tears would not stop. My uncle didn't hesitate and said, "I'm on my way!" I knew it was going to be ugly when my uncle found Willie.

Getting out of the house was my best bet. I knew I could run into the streets if Willie tried to come after me. My uncle's car could be heard coming down the street, full speed. Willie had crossed the street headed to my mom's car as my uncle pulled up in his car to the house. I was standing on the porch waiting for him afraid to go back into the house by myself.

My uncle must have seen Willie about to get into the car. He instantly pushed the gas pedal to the medal to go faster and tried to run him over. Fortunately for Willie, he was so drunk he saw the car coming and fell over a fire hydrant away from the oncoming vehicle. That did not stop my uncle from getting out of his car and beating the living crap out of Willie.

My uncle beat Willie so bad, my mother was pissed. Pissed to the point she called me a liar. She would not believe Willie molested me. "So, you'd go in front of a judge and tell them my husband molested you?" She was truly tripping. Asking a child that question. "Yes, ma'am I sure would." Was my response. "Well, you was probably walking around half ass naked. Any man would get aroused by a young girl half naked. You need to learn how to dress respectfully in my damn house and around my husband. You little tramp!"

My heart dropped. Her words hurt. But what hurt more was that she believed I would lie on her drunk husband. A husband that beat her almost every other day!

The police were never called, and the molestation was swept under the table so to speak. I held in the hurt and pain. I had nowhere else to go. I felt stuck.

Chapter 25

"Tatianna, can I borrow your bell bottom pants?"
"No, I already told you, Tina."

I didn't feel like lending Tina my bell bottoms again. Not that I wanted to wear them, because I didn't. Ever since the last time, Tina borrowed them, and I saw how much better they fit her, I no longer wanted to wear them or see her wear them. Truth be told. Tina was a chocolate drop of beauty. Her dark skin was smooth and clear. She was short, petite and shapely. Tina has dark long thick hair. We all inherited good hair from our mother. Her most unattractive feature was her nose. It didn't seem to fit her pretty face. It was big! Fortunately for her, no one ever noticed it enough to make fun of her but ME!

"Come on, little sis, please."

"No. and I'm not going to tell you again."

I rolled my eyes. Tina isn't going to give up. She never gives up. Out of the three of us girls, Tina favored our biological mother the most. She would always get her way. My baby sister and I caught pure hell. She would get us in trouble whenever it looked as if she wasn't going to have her way.

Lending her my bell bottom pants was out of the question.

Tina asked me again, just like I thought and again I said no.

We were growing apart at a rapid rate. It was inevitable when we entered high school at Andrew Jackson. No one would believe we were sisters because we went our separate ways. It was as if we lead another life. As if we had multiple personalities---- one for our mom, a second for the projects, and a third for school.

As we entered high school, I no longer cared about Tina having her way. I wanted to be free from our dysfunctional family. We had been put together like a puzzle and one of the most important pieces of the puzzle was missing, our deceased mother. And I wanted out. I asked to be emancipated. I wanted my freedom. The answer was no. The answer was no, not because my mom/aunt really loved and wanted me to stay. She wanted to continue receiving the check she would get monthly from our biological mother's death. She could have the check I was going to have it my way for a change.

Jacksonville, Florida was hot as fire the first-day Jaheim, a local dope boy stepped to me with his proposition to hustle drugs. Hey, I was on *"GO"* before he could say, *"On your mark, get ready, set."* Anything to get away from the miserable home life I lived. The authorities would call it running away. I called it freedom away from prison. And all the while I was running, Jesus was running side by side with me. He knew I reached out in all the wrong places because I never saw right.

It wasn't long before my Boss brother Jaheim placed me on his payroll. I learned how to cook, bag, and sell dope. My popularity as the *"HOT GIRL"* had other females hunting me down so they could hang out with me. I would get dropped off in the front of the school in the morning, only to walk to the back of the school to be picked up by one of the dope boys I called brothers.

The dope boys were older and had money. I would count the money for them and sell every type of drug they pushed.

My girlfriends, of course, believed I was living the good life and wanted to meet my brothers. Obviously, the only meeting my brothers were interested in with my girlfriends was sex. Initially, I had a heart. I felt responsible for my girlfriends and wouldn't allow them to turn the girls out.

However, that changed when my brothers offered me money. I saw myself as a **side-pimp**. I would round up different girls and take them to the **hang out** spot during the week. Dope boys, and round the way girls would show up and watch the dope boys drive through in their **Box Chevy** cars while they played loud music. They would show off during lunch time to see which girl would take the bait. Most girls wanted a dope boy or a bad boy. Dope boys wanted money and sex. Sex is, and always has been a commodity, and as such falls prey to the laws of supply and demand.

Hormones were a force to be reckoned with for teenagers. Some of my girlfriends were stacked like a stallion. And my brothers would say, "I want that one right there with that big ole' **onion booty**!" Or "That one right there, is collard green, cornbread, well-fed thick!" Some of the old heads sat across the street at the corner store played checkers and drank beer and some more dope boys rounded the block on bikes, searching for their next lick.

The majority of the dope boys was tied down to some chick, but on the prowl for some fresh, young pu'nanny. My Boss brother Jaheim, was always in demand. The girls always wanted the one with the power. He was a swirl baby, a mixture of Caucasian and African American. His big puff was pulled into a ponytail and tucked into a ball at the top of his head. His neatly trimmed beard outlined his sexy lips that were nice, full, and pink. Jaheim was casually dressed in a white t-shirt, jean shorts and a pair of all-white **Air Force Ones** looking real sexy!

My girl Shaunie stared too hard because he rounded the corner in the 2000 smoke grey Chevy Impala he drove.

"What's good, Tatianna?" he spoke and gave Shaunie direct eye contact. The way his golds gleamed with every word he spoke had my girl Shaunie in a trance. "Just chilling, you?" I replied while Shaunie licked her already glossy lips at him. "I'm just on the block handling my business. You good?" he asked. "I'm good." He looked at Shaunie and said, "What's your name shorty? You need a ride?" She tried to act like she wasn't interested. "Boy, I don't know you like that."

"You don't, but it's hot as hell. I've been on this block for an hour, so I can tell you ya'll just missed the bus and got about forty minutes before the next one come." He smirked.

"Why you running game? Shaunie quizzed.

"I'm not. You too damn thick to be sitting in this heat, wit cho fine azz" He added with an LL Cool J style lip of his own. I shook my head because Jaheim had true game. "Hey ya'll I'm out. I see my ride pulling up. I gotta go make that paper. I'll see ya'll around." I looked at Shaunie and said, "You gonna be alright? I'm headed to the Westside." She whispered to me "It's whatever. I got my mace, so we good," she replied. "All right...," I whispered to Shaunie. "I'm out!" I yelled over to Jaheim and threw up the deuce sign. His dope boy flip phone rang, he answered it and walked away toward his ride with Shaunie. He might have been half-white, but he had hood etched all over him.

Chapter 26

I couldn't catch freedom if it paid me. My mom would find me herself or she'd call the police. "Girl, you are gonna be the death of me if I let you. I ain't trying to die." My mom would go on and on once she found me and got me home from the streets. "You ain't never gonna be nothing if you keep hanging out in the streets." I would stand still and listen to the name calling and take the beatings because I knew I'd leave again. I hated my life with my abusive mom (Aunt Yvonne) We would continue to play *come and get me.* Because I wasn't staying!

"Your ass gonna end up in prison, just like your sorry behind daddy. Keep running the streets Tatianna." I would try and tune her out. She kept on. "Your daddy ain't no good. He can't stay out of jail and you following in his footsteps." She pointed her finger at me. You ain't gonna graduate from high school either. He was a dropout and you're headed in that same direction." She went to the refrigerator and retrieved a beer. She popped the lid and said, "You headed down that same path. You might as well not go to school period!"

I thought that was the best advice she could give me. I hated school. I always fought when I did go, and I cut school when I wanted to hang out with my Boss brother Jaheim. I felt accomplished when I was doing something for me and making money was doing something for Tatianna. I made money without being cursed out, neither was I being abused mentally or physically when I hustled dope. I felt my freedom was going to come at a real cost. What the cost would be I had no idea.

I found myself praying a lot more. I really didn't believe God cared. I mean, how could he let the abuse happen to me and my sisters? I would lay in bed at night and pray. I would pray so hard until I would fall asleep praying. My prayers seemed to turn into dreams. My dreams always answered whatever I would talk to God about.

The most amazing part of each dream is that the dreams would always start out with my mom smiling. But this night my mom wasn't smiling in the dream. She sat on the bed in her bedroom. She held a sawed-off shot gun in her hand and it was pointed toward my dad. She was small in size and looked uncomfortable as she held the weapon in her hands.

In the dream, my mother described to me what happened the day of her murder.

Destiny: I was packing my clothes to leave. I wanted to take Tina and Terrie to my mom's house because you were already there. Your dad and I had argued so much during the week about his late nights out. Staying out all night and not having enough money to take care of us. He would blow the money and I would either have to work overtime leaving the three of you with a relative or with your dad who I felt loved you in his own way but didn't show it as a father should. I was at the end of my rope. I tried everything I could to make it work. I was tired.

I emptied the dresser drawers of my clothes and placed them in a large duffel bag. Your dad walked in. **"Where the hell do**

you think you going?" *I continued to push items into the duffel bag. I ignored your dad. When he was angry he was a force to be reckoned with. I tried to shake off his overnight stays by having breakfast prepared when he got home that morning. Your dad loved to eat and breakfast was really his favorite meal when he was home. I had hoped we could resolve our differences. But, I didn't want to play the victim anymore. I wanted to get out and move on with my babies.*

"You ain't going nowhere. You can put that ish, right back." *I looked at him and said,* **"It's over. You don't respect or appreciate me or the babies. Listen to you. Arguing and screaming at me knowing they are asleep.** *He tried to grab the duffel bag away from me. I said,* **"I'm tired of you and your crap! I'?"m taking my babies and you can stay out as long as you want to from now on!"**

Before I could move away, he slapped me as hard as I had ever been slapped by him. It wasn't the first time. I pushed him away from me with all the strength that I could muster. He shoved me so hard I fell on the floor and hit my head. He walked out of the room. I knew where we kept the shotgun your granddaddy gave us. I struggled to get up from the floor and went to the closet to get the gun.

I'd barely touched a gun before that night. I don't know how I did it. I only felt my breath go out of me and I waited for him to come back into the room. He was not going to hit me another time. I didn't care! I sat on the bed waiting for him to come back with the gun pointed at the door. Right before he entered the room my emotions took over my thoughts, and my mind was all over the place. **"Should I kill him, or should I injure him? He is the father of your children and your husband. You are going to jail either way. Don't do it, do it!"** *Everything inside of me shook. I knew one thing I was going to shoot him if he didn't back away and let me leave with my babies.*

I looked up and Andre was already coming through the door at me. **"So, you think you gonna shoot me Destiny?"** *My hands trembled, tears flooded my eyes. I tried to pull the trigger, I felt weak. Andre' reached for the gun. I was trying to hold on to the gun to throw it on the floor, so no one would get hurt. Andre's strength overpowered me, I fell back onto the bed as he forced the gun from my hand and pointed it in my direction.*

The flaming hot bullet hit me in the head. I was pushed back from the impact of the bullet as Andre stared at me in shock. I seem to be able to see my body, I see myself. Laying there, so still. I am dead. Being murdered by your husband is indescribable. People always wonder what death feels like, and now I know. It's

Peaceful l... never wanted to leave my babies. Anger, lust, and pain took me away from the only thing I lived for my children.

When I awoke I shivered under the blankets that were over me. I cried uncontrollably. I wasn't there at two, but in the spirit realm, God showed me exactly how our mother was murdered. She was murdered by our father and he seemed to have gotten away. That dream changed my entire life.

"There is a time for everything and a season for everything under the heavens. Ecclesiastes 3:1

A change had to come. I lay in bed and cried my heart out. I wanted to change. I wanted my life to be different and I didn't want to end up like my dad. I wanted to be seen in a positive way. Not negative. That night God whispered his love into my ears. He told me everything was going to be alright. I didn't know when or how it would happen I simply believed!

Chapter 27

OF course every girl remembers her *first cut*. In layman's terms that would be my *first love*. His name was Darrell. I was 15 and he was a 17. I liked him because he talked to me and seemed interesting and funny. He always gave me compliments. He was kind. I gave him my telephone number and then waited, my heart pounding, for him to call, which he did the next day.

We arranged to go hang out. I had been out with boys before. I had the dope boyfriend when I hustled drugs. I went out with him only because he had a car.

But Darrell, he was different. He was kind, caring and protective. He wanted the simple things in life. I enjoyed being with someone that enjoyed being with me for me. I was comfortable around him. He made me feel safe. In all honesty we discovered deep emotions. He made me smile and truth be told, I was desperate at the same time for a real love.

It was as if I had to learn a whole new lexicon for my life. He made my heart heave. He could make me smile and cry within one sentence and I would find myself staring at him for hours on end and him at me. I marveled at how this beautiful young man loved me.

And we discovered sex. Not just fumbling, unwanted sex in the back of a car, but real, passionate sex where we spent time and energy with each other, both naïve but willing and trusting. There was no abuse. He showed me the utmost respect. I was so grateful and thankful to God for answered prayers.

After the last argument my mother and I had about school I dropped out. I lied on an application at Taco Bell and got a job. Darrell and I got our first apartment and moved in together.

Life was stable for us. We had each other. I worked and took care of the necessary bills we had to pay together. It wasn't just fifty-fifty. We were on a mission to make it.

With Darrell and I moving on and going forward. We were determined to live of good solid, stable lifestyle. We would work and support each other. Something I never had because our mother was never able to be the stable adult she was supposed to be. She was evicted from her place and guess who she ran to? Me.

The phone rang three times before I answered. I was just getting in from work. "Tatianna, it's mom. How you are doing?" I answered slowly, thinking of what reason she would have to call me. Was somebody sick or dead? I finally said, "I'm fine mom. How are you?" She sighed, and said, "We've been evicted and need a place to stay. Can we come and camp out with you and Darrell for a couple of weeks? I know it's short notice, but I'm out of places to stay in the family." I hesitated and said, "Let me talk with Darrell first and I'll call you back when he gets off from work tonight."

"Thank you, Tatianna, Call me back OK?"

"I said, I would mom." I hung up. "Dang she wants me to be there for her, but she was never there for me." I thought of a scripture I often read.

The 23 *Psalm: **Thou preparest a table before me in the presence of mine enemies: thou anointest my head with oil; my cup runneth over.***

    I will make you enemies your foot stool.

    Darrell agreed to allow my mom and family to stay with us temporarily. Her husband was estranged, and my sisters and mom moved into our apartment. We put up with my mother and two sisters as well as one of my sister's boyfriend living with us.

    Darrell and I both were working two jobs while they laid up and enjoyed the fruits of our labor. They took advantage of the situation and we got tired of it. We allowed the electricity to be cut off and sure enough my mom and sisters bounced! They left without saying good bye.

Chapter 28

Not long after my mom and sisters moved out of my apartment I ran into my father. We bumped into each other at the Regency Square Mall. I was in line at the food court about to purchase my meal. I felt a tap on my shoulder. I turned to look at the person who tapped me on my shoulder. It was my dad. I jumped at his touch. My eyes grew wide. Words would not find their way from my head to my mouth.

"Hey baby girl, I thought that was you when I walked up to the line. How you doing?" I wanted to slap his face the way he slapped my mother. I wanted to curse him out using words unfit for the human ear. I also wanted to be held by a father that would protect me, take away all the misery I had gone through and most of all to tell me he was sorry. Instead I say. "I'm doing good." He went on to say, "Well, just got out of jail yesterday and came to the mall with an old friend of mine to do some shopping." I'm looking at this man, a stranger to me and a murderer from my mother's dreams. I am at a loss for words. I stare. He goes on to ask me, "You out here with you sisters? I'd love to see them too." I finally found words to convey my thoughts, "So, you just got out? My sisters aren't with me. I'm on my lunch break." He looked down and said, "Well,

I'm trying to find a job and I don't have any money. Could you spare your dad a little sumptin, sumptin?"

I immediately think of the dream. I couldn't believe he was never charged with the murder of my mother. He always found a way to go to jail for petty crimes. That didn't seem to make me feel better about what he did to my mother. But I didn't want to add injury to insult. I had just gotten paid. "I got a few dollars I can give to you." I handed him some cash and said, "That's all I got. Hope everything works out for you." He looked at the money first and said, "Thanks baby girl. I'll pay you back." He walked away. No hug, no how can I reach you later. He only wanted what he could get from me a little *sumptin, sumptin* and he was satisfied.

Darrell and I soon parted ways after years of trying to make life good for us. We didn't have any animosity between each other. We simply grew apart.

In comes Avery, he had more baby momma drama than a movie. His aggressive personality frightened me. I was trapped once by my adopted mom. I wasn't going through that situation again.

Avery was a beast when he wanted sex. We would fight and that only made matters worse. But, for some reason I couldn't walk away. I eventually ended up pregnant. This event in my life made me feel trapped. I watched my adopted mother go through this type of relationship for years. The generational curse was not going to be a part of my life. I rebuked it in the name of Jesus!

Even with Avery and I using protection, I was feeling bad, queasy and unable to keep my food down.

Avery admitted he poked holes in the condoms. I went for a second pregnancy test. It was confirmed. I was pregnant. The first thing I do is tell Avery and this negro denies he could be the father! What the ham fat?"

Avery looks at me in disgust and said, "It ain't my baby. You ain't pinning it on me!" I'm like, "You can't be serious?" He admitted poking holes into the condoms and I simply did what any woman with a tad bit of sense would do, walk away I tried not to look back, but I did.

Chapter 29

I'm 18 ears old, expecting a baby, single, uneducated, and still, involved with a baby daddy. Through the chaos of life, I tried to do positive things. I went back to school. I would become depressed and not eat. Avery was abusive during the pregnancy.

Avery would come home and ask, "Where the hell is dinner Tatianna? Just because you having a baby don't mean you can't cook." He would slap me around and I would cry until I ached. I was trapped. Avery was like a Dr. Jekyll and Mr. Hyde. One day he loved me, the next day he hated me.

I decided to end the relationship and that was the straw that broke the camel back. Avery tried to set my face on fire. I refused to bring a baby into the world under the conditions I lived.

Finally, after two years of torment I was able to get away from Avery. I was free! My child was two years old when I met who I thought was my prince charming! He was handsome, polite, smart and so nice to me at the beginning. Mike was his name. He turned on me and showed me another side. He needed a woman that would cater to him. I got pregnant again. This time I had a baby girl. I went from the fire to the frying pan in my relationships with men.

Mike had a baby from me and two other women. Talk about drama! He was an emotional abuser. He was never physical while I was pregnant, but he never ceased the emotional abuse with his words.

Three to four times a week after our daughter was born I was dealt physical abuse. We would fight like cats and dogs. My self-esteem was at zero. Therefore, I tolerated any abuse I was dealt.

I went through having DNA tests with a man that slept with me nightly. and refused to acknowledge he was the father of our baby. I was so messed up!

To the point I really felt what my mother must have felt when she got tired of being sick and tired of my father's abuse.

Mike was the last of the **Mohicans.** I wasn't going to allow my children to watch their mother go down the road of manipulation and abuse by a man. I understood life dealt me a hand that seemed to be a losing hand, but I knew God didn't make no junk. I understand that I didn't have to put a permanent stamp on a temporary situation. I knew in my heart that *the prayers of the righteous man availeth much.*

I got to the point where I just couldn't imagine spending the rest of my life with Mike. At some point, **I wished that he would die** because I felt *How am I going to get out of this relationship? There's no way I'm going to leave alive.*

I would fantasize about seeing him dead, but I would feel awful thinking about it. Until he did the unthinkable. He drew a gun on me. It reminded me of my mother's murder. He was bluffing. He didn't go through with it. But it frightened me enough to know I was not going to live that type of lifestyle of being in fear. He was very capable and able to kill me. I didn't want my children to end up motherless as I did.

Mike was so intoxicated on this night, he ranted and raved about killing me and my child. That wasn't going to happen. I revisited the dream from my mother's murder and I prayed. *"Lord I reverse the curse in the name of Jesus on my life and my children's life. No weapon formed against us shall prosper.* Mike attempted to harm me first with abusive words. He was so intoxicated, when he fell asleep on the sofa, I decided to roll him up in the mat I used to do exercise on after having our daughter. Fortunately for me, and for Mike, he didn't die. I could be in prison right now. Fortunately, for me, God saw a way out of no way. I have been redeemed.

I was given a second chance through the grace of God. My life has been a testimony from the test I took. I am able to share the "Good News" with those who have found themselves in the trenches of abuse, the Foster Care system and molestation.

I am blessed and fortunate enough to have been redeemed by the blood of the lamb. Saved, sanctified, and filled with the Holy Ghost. Ordained as a Prophetess. Married to a Godly man that adores me and our children. Spreading the gospel to a lost and dying world.

It hasn't been easy. Life continues to have the trials and the tribulations we were told in the living Word would come. Through God and with God, all things are possible.

My healing has come and forgiveness to release those who allowed the enemy to use them to push me to my destiny I say "THANK YOU. YOU ARE FORGIVEN."

It's never easy to face the challenges God allows to be placed in our lives. But remember, when the heat of trials in our life and tribulations seem too hot to bear and the temperature is turned up to HIGH, just remember who controls the temperature. GOD!

Blessings and peace to you. I pray this book will help you to become the overcomer in every area the enemy has challenged you to doubt God!

Prophetess, Tyeashia Ansley- Hughes Neeley

Tyeashia Ansley-Hughes Neeley resides in Jacksonville, Florida with her Husband and children. For booking information e-mail the author: Tyeashianeeley@gmail.com

www.ingramcontent.com/pod-product-compliance
Lightning Source LLC
Chambersburg PA
CBHW071315110426
42743CB00042B/2554